THE BEST BOOK OF

Early People

Margaret Hynes

KINGFISHER

Contents

KINGFISHER

a Houghton Mifflin Company imprint
222 Berkeley Street
Boston, Massachusetts 02116
www.houghtonmifflinbooks.com

Created for Kingfisher Publications Plc
by Picthall & Gunzi Limited

Author: Margaret Hynes
Designer: Dominic Zwemmer
Editor: Lauren Robertson
Consultant: Philip Wilkinson
Illustrators: Michael White, Peter Ross,
   Marion Appleton, Angus McBride

First published by Kingfisher
Publications Plc 2003

10 9 8 7 6 5 4 3 2 1

1TR/0203/WKT/GLG(GLG)/128KMA

LIBRARY OF CONGRESS CATALOGING-IN-PUBLICATION DATA
has been applied for.

ISBN 0-7534-5577-3

Printed in Hong Kong

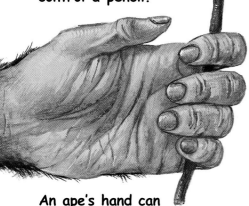

A human's hand can control a pencil.

An ape's hand can only grasp objects.

Fingers and thumbs

Humans can pinch objects between their thumb and forefinger. This means that they can make things using their hands. Apes have short thumbs, so they can hold objects but cannot make things.

Meet the humans

The first humanlike creatures are known as "hominids," and many scientists believe that they had the same ancestors as apes. The first hominid, called *Australopithecus*, lived in Africa between five and one million years ago. Over several million years hominids learned to walk upright. Their brains also grew larger over time.

The march through time

The first apes lived 30 million years ago, and the first hominids lived around five million years ago. A long time ago apes and hominids looked similar, but they evolved, or developed, separately.

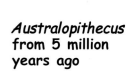

Proconsul
25 million
years ago

Pliopithecus
15 million
years ago

Australopithecus
from 5 million
years ago

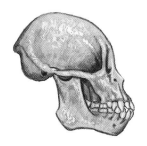 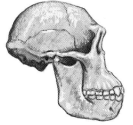 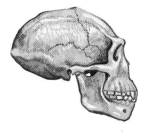 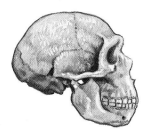 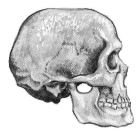

Proconsul *Australopithecus* *Homo erectus* *Neanderthal* *Homo sapiens*

Bigger heads for bigger brains

Archaeologists have found skulls that show that the brains
of hominids gradually got bigger over millions of years. As their
brains grew hominids were able to do more difficult tasks. They
began to make tools, build shelters, use fire, and hunt for food.

Homo habilis
from 2 million
years ago

Homo erectus
from 1.8 million
years ago

Neanderthal
from 100,000 to
35,000 years ago

Homo sapiens
from 1 million
years ago to today

The first toolmakers

Two million years ago a species of *Australopithecus* developed into a hominid called *Homo*. *Homo* had a bigger brain and a more humanlike face than *Australopithecus*. The earliest species of *Homo* could make stone tools and huts in which to live. This group was called *Homo habilis*, which means "handy man."

Handy man

As their brains grew in size *Homo habilis* were able to do more difficult tasks. This species also had hands that could grip objects, so *Homo habilis* could make simple tools. They were able to build shelters from tree branches, leaves, and stones, like those shown in the camp below.

Large stones kept the branches of the shelter in place.

Finding food

Australopithecus lived in trees. They came down to the ground to find plants to eat or to gather berries (right). *Homo habilis* lived on the ground. They ate plants and meat. *Homo habilis* may also have eaten the meat from dead animals that were abandoned by predators.

Australopithecus gathering berries

Bones from scavenged carcasses could be found in *Homo habilis* settlements.

Homo habilis used stones to make simple tools in order to cut meat from carcasses.

Walking upright

A hominid called *Homo erectus*, or "upright man," lived between 1.8 million and 200,000 years ago.

Homo erectus gradually moved from Africa into China. They learned to use fire, so they were able to survive in Europe, which at that time was covered in ice. *Homo erectus* had bigger brains than *Homo habilis*. They lived in caves and made many different tools.

A group of *Homo erectus* skins a dead animal.

Making fire

At first *Homo erectus* used fires that were caused naturally by lightning. Later they may have learned how to make fires by rubbing sticks together or by striking stones to make a spark. They put stones around a fire to stop it from spreading and to protect it from the wind.

Keeping warm

Homo erectus family groups gathered together around fires to stay warm. They probably also made fires to cook meat and to frighten away wild animals. Sometimes hunters also used fire to force animals into traps.

8

A *Homo erectus* family group keeps warm around a fire.

Storing berries

The Neanderthals

From 100,000 years ago a type of *Homo sapiens* called Neanderthals lived in Europe, Asia, and Africa. They had stocky bodies and brains as large as those humans have today. During their lifetime Europe and Asia were covered with ice. Neanderthals learned how to survive in the cold by making clothes from animal hides, or skins, by living in caves, and by using fire.

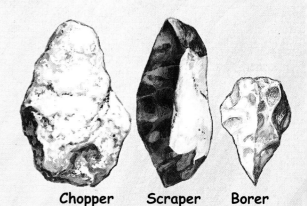

Chopper   Scraper   Borer

Early tools
The Neanderthals made different tools for scraping, cutting, and making holes in hides. These early toolmakers needed patience and practice to make stone and flint tools.

Animal horns were placed on top of graves.

Neanderthal burials

The Neanderthals may have been the first hominids to care for their sick and to bury their dead. They placed flowers around a dead body and marked the grave with animal horns.

Neanderthals placed flowers in graves.

The first tools

Hammerstone

Core

Homo habilis made simple tools by knocking small pieces off of stones in order to form sharp edges. Later people made more complicated tools from a stone called flint. They made the tools by removing flakes from a piece of flint until it had a pointed edge. This is how hand axes were made. People also used the small flakes to make sharper tools, like knives and scrapers.

Making a hand ax

1 First the toolmaker chose a piece of flint called the core. A hammerstone was used to knock large pieces off of the flint.

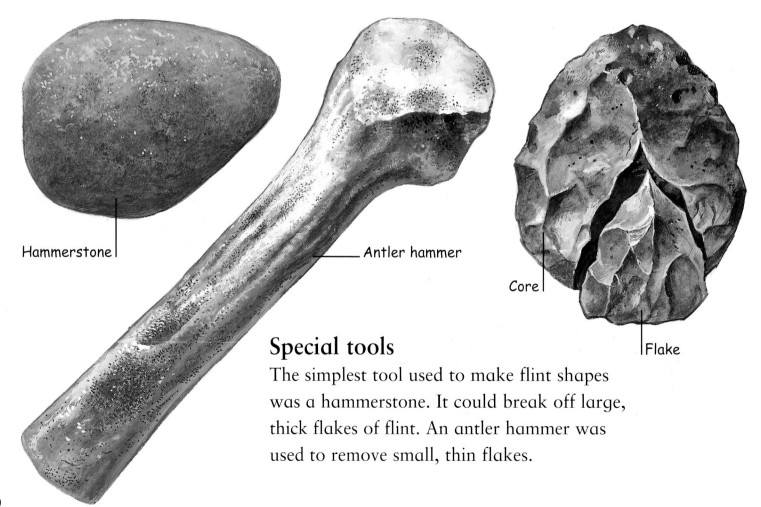

Hammerstone

Antler hammer

Core

Flake

Special tools

The simplest tool used to make flint shapes was a hammerstone. It could break off large, thick flakes of flint. An antler hammer was used to remove small, thin flakes.

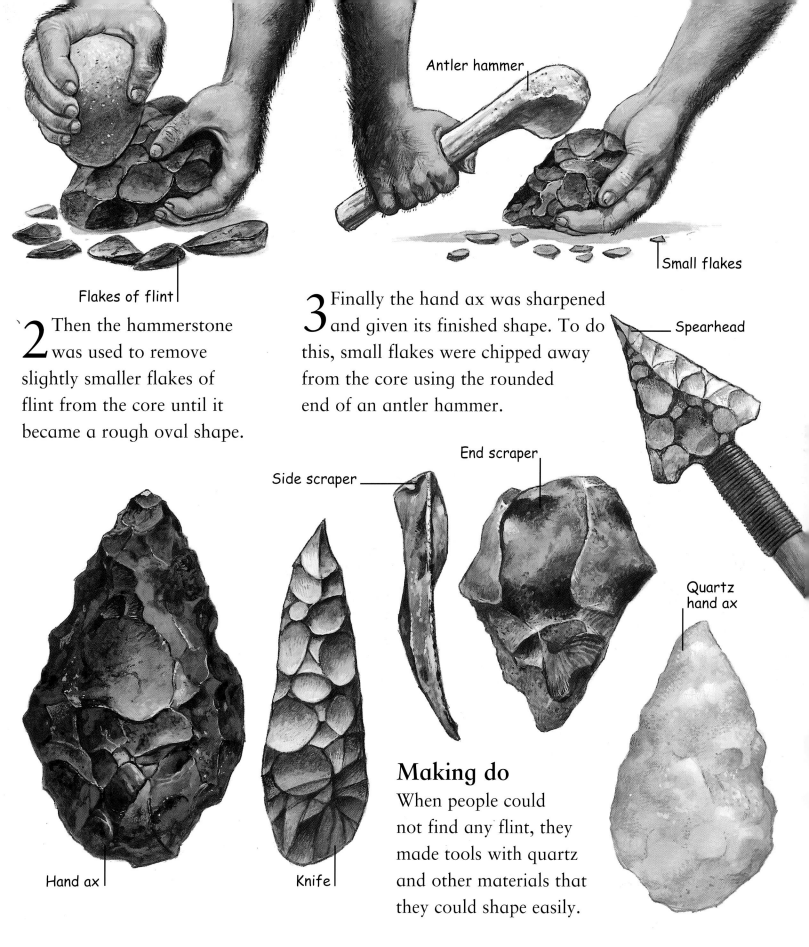

Antler hammer

Small flakes

Flakes of flint

2 Then the hammerstone was used to remove slightly smaller flakes of flint from the core until it became a rough oval shape.

3 Finally the hand ax was sharpened and given its finished shape. To do this, small flakes were chipped away from the core using the rounded end of an antler hammer.

Spearhead

Side scraper

End scraper

Quartz hand ax

Hand ax

Knife

Making do

When people could not find any flint, they made tools with quartz and other materials that they could shape easily.

13

Our early ancestors

Archaeologists believe that _Homo sapiens_ first lived in Africa and then moved across the world.
This group was called _Homo sapiens_, or "wise man," because they had larger brains than earlier species and because they learned to live in different climates. _Homo sapiens_ are our early ancestors, and they first lived around one million years ago.

Living well

Early _Homo sapiens_ hunted animals, such as mammoths, and used the meat, skin, and bones. They built homes from tree branches and animal skins in order to shelter from the cold. They also fished for food and made tools from wood, flint, and bones.

This group of _Homo sapiens_ hunters lived in southern Russia.

On the move

By 100,000 years ago *Homo sapiens* lived in southern and eastern Africa. From there they traveled hundreds of miles to the Middle East. By 11,000 years ago *Homo sapiens* had reached the Americas.

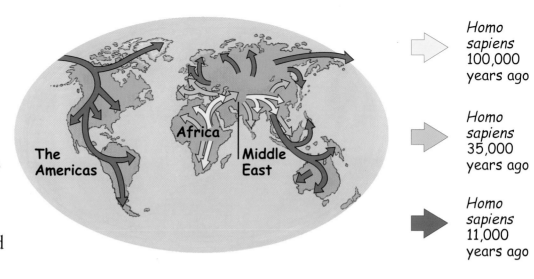

Homo sapiens 100,000 years ago

Homo sapiens 35,000 years ago

Homo sapiens 11,000 years ago

Homo sapiens built shelters from branches and animal skins.

The women scraped the animal skins clean.

Working together

During the last Ice Age our ancestors worked in groups to hunt and capture large animals such as woolly mammoths. They dug pits to trap an animal, and once it was caught, they killed it with sharp spears.

Hunters trap a woolly mammoth.

Mammoths were forced into pits by the hunters.

Life in the last Ice Age

Between 32,000 and 10,000 years ago parts of the earth's surface were covered with ice. Cold periods like this are known as ice ages. Life was difficult for early humans during this last Ice Age. Some food plants could not grow, and there was very little wood for shelters. People had to find new foods, such as fish, and new building materials such as animal bones.

New types of food

Early hunters learned how to track animals that lived in herds such as reindeer. They used harpoons to kill seals and to catch fish in the icy rivers.

Bone sewing needle

Antler harpoon head

Ax made from stone and antlers

Bone and antler tools

During the Ice Age people used more bone and reindeer antlers than their ancestors. They made sewing needles from carved bone and used antlers to make handles for stone axes.

x

17

Early artists

The earliest pictures were painted 30,000 years ago during the last Ice Age. The first artists painted these pictures on rocks and on the walls and roofs of caves. People also made sculptures using bone and clay. This early artwork can be found in many parts of the world. It tells us a lot about how our ancestors lived at that time and about the animals that they hunted.

Australian art

Early artists in Australia painted colorful pictures of animals, rivers, and rocks. They believed their ancestors became these things when they died.

Natural colors

Early artists made colored paints using minerals in the soil and in rocks. Chalk was used to make white paint, charcoal made black, and iron oxide made red. Brushes or pads of animal hair were used to apply paint to rocks.

Iron oxide

Chalk

Charcoal

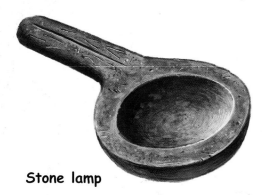

Stone lamp

Seeing in the dark

Artists often worked deep inside caves where there was no light. They burned animal fat in stone lamps so that they could see what they were doing.

Animal fat in stone dish

This artist
holds a stone
lamp to light up
the cave wall.

European rock art

The most famous rock paintings
are in caves in Lascaux in France
(shown here) and Altimira in Spain.
Some paintings show hunting scenes,
and others show herds of animals
such as cattle, horses, and reindeer.
Archaeologists think these works
of art may be 17,000 years old.

A time of plenty

The last Ice Age ended around 10,000 years ago. Over time forests developed and replaced the melting ice. New types of plants and animals evolved and lived in the forests, so our ancestors did not have to travel as far to find food. This gave people more time to make better tools. They ate well and lived longer, and the world's population increased.

Settling down

People began to stay in one place for longer periods of time, so they built their homes to last. Hunters in Siberia (below) made shelters using animal bones and tusks, which they covered with animal hides.

The hunters cooked animals over an open fire.

Making bread

As the ice thawed in Africa and Asia some areas became covered in grasses. People gathered the grasses and then separated the seeds from the stalks. They ground the seeds into flour and mixed the flour with water. The mixture was baked to make flat cakes of bread.

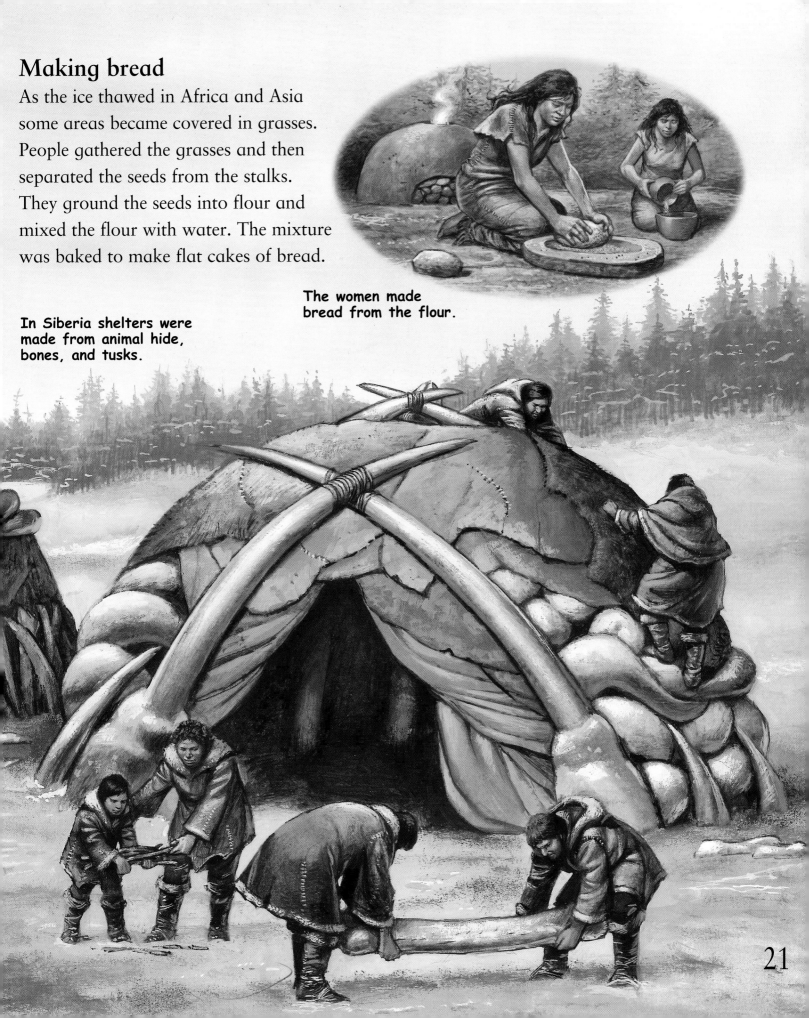

The women made bread from the flour.

In Siberia shelters were made from animal hide, bones, and tusks.

The first farmers

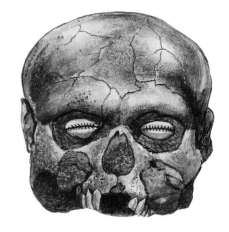

Groups of hunters around the world gradually learned how to farm. At first they may have collected wild crops such as wheat. They also began to round up herds of the wild animals that they hunted. By 11,000 years ago the first farmers were planting and growing their own crops in the Middle East. People also began to keep and breed different types of animals for milk and meat.

New styles of art

Farming was hard work, but people still found time to develop new styles of art. This human skull would have been covered in plaster and used in ceremonies.

This farming settlement in Turkey grew crops and herded animals.

Early farmers usually shared their homes with their animals.

An animal called a wild aurochs was the early ancestor of cattle.

22

Breeding crops and animals

Early farmers knew how to grow, or farm, the best crops. They took seeds from the biggest plants in a crop and sowed them in order to grow larger plants the next year. They also chose the healthiest animals for breeding.

Early farming towns

Farmers became rich, and they built more houses that were larger and grouped together. These groups of houses eventually grew into the first villages, towns, and cities.

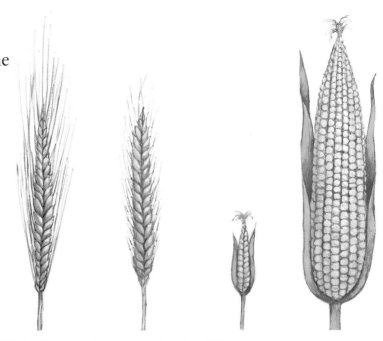

Wild wheat **Farmed wheat** **Wild corn** **Farmed corn**

23

The Bronze Age

From around 5,500 years ago people in western Asia began using a metal called bronze to make tools and weapons. This period is called the Bronze Age. Bronze was formed by melting copper and tin together. It was harder and more durable than other metals. Metalworking was a full-time job, so farmers had to grow enough food to feed all of the metalworkers, too.

Casting bronze

Early metalworkers made bronze objects by a method called casting. First bronze bars were melted. Then the hot metal was poured into a mold and allowed to cool and set. Bronze could be cast into different shapes. Casting was done in a special area, away from the houses.

Stone molds for making pins to wear in clothes

A sign of wealth

Bronze was expensive because copper and tin were hard to find. At first only rich people could afford to buy bronze. They used bronze objects, such as jewelry and weapons, to show off their wealth.

Sword

Spear

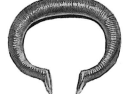

Razor

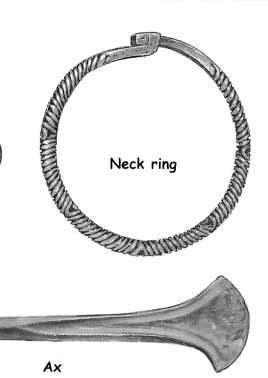

Neck ring

Bracelet

Ax

This man is preparing copper and tin for melting.

It took two men to pour the heavy melted bronze into the mold.

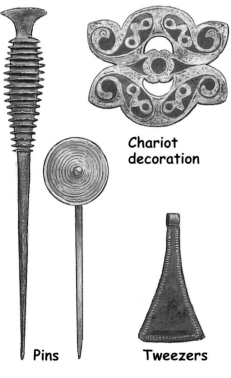

Pins

Chariot decoration

Tweezers

Village life

More and more people wanted bronze objects so groups of metalworkers began to sell the things that they made. They set up trading centers that developed into small villages. These settlements were often built close to rivers, where the rich soil was also good for farming.

25

Life in the Iron Age

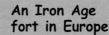

The metal that we call iron was discovered in the Middle East around 3,300 years ago. People began to make weapons and other objects using iron, and ironworking soon spread to Europe. Some groups of people, such as the Celts, used iron weapons to fight other peoples and to take over their lands. The Celts become very powerful in this way. They built hill forts that were large enough for people, houses, and herds of animals.

An Iron Age
fort in Europe

Building walls

The Celts protected their forts by surrounding them with deep ditches. The earth from the ditches was used to make high barriers that gave extra protection. Iron weapons were then used to fight off any attackers.

Huge gate
to protect the
fort's entrance

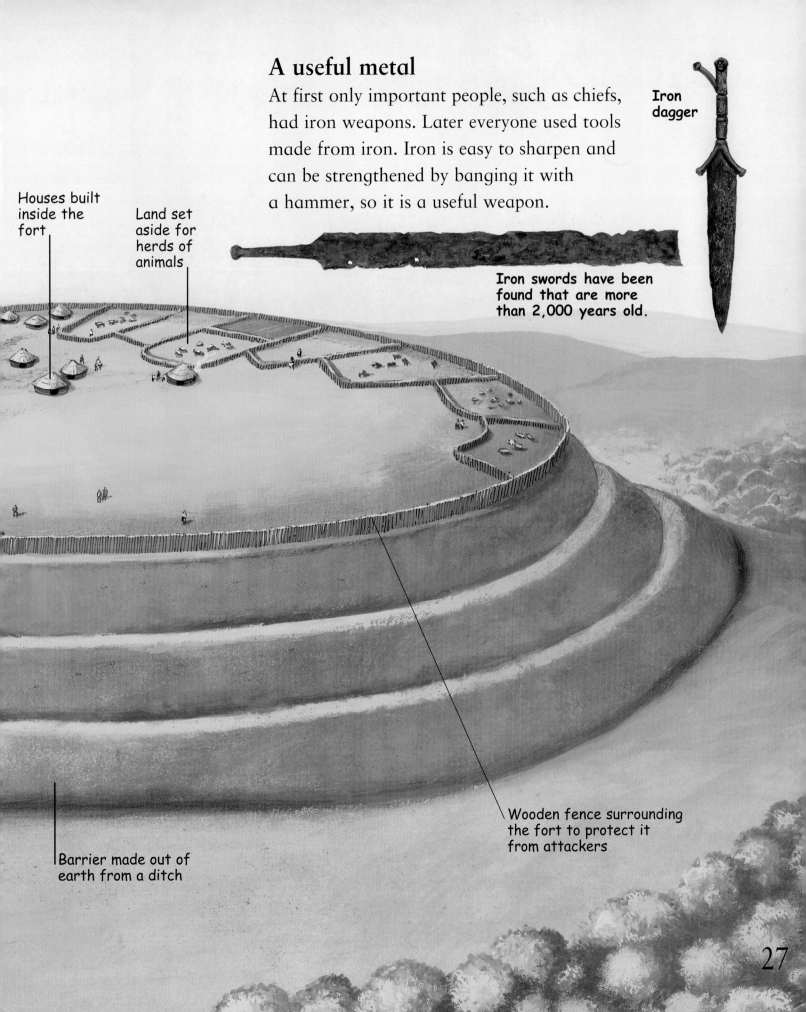

A useful metal

At first only important people, such as chiefs, had iron weapons. Later everyone used tools made from iron. Iron is easy to sharpen and can be strengthened by banging it with a hammer, so it is a useful weapon.

Iron dagger

Iron swords have been found that are more than 2,000 years old.

Houses built inside the fort

Land set aside for herds of animals

Wooden fence surrounding the fort to protect it from attackers

Barrier made out of earth from a ditch

Civilization begins

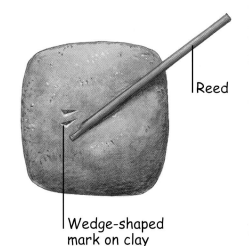

Around 8,000 years ago towns began to develop into cities. The people who lived in these cities built temples and palaces and began to write things down. In these communities there were many different jobs for people to do. This new way of life in the city is what we now call civilization. Civilization began in an area of the Middle East called Mesopotamia.

Cuneiform

The people of Mesopotamia wrote by making marks in clay tablets with a wedge-shaped reed. This writing is called cuneiform, which means "wedge" in Greek.

Reed

Wedge-shaped mark on clay

First letters

Writing was invented in Mesopotamia around 5,200 years ago. At first people wrote down lists of the things that they traded. Soon they started to write down stories.

28

The people of Mesopotamia

Mesopotamians became wealthy by farming and trading. In the city of Ur rich people filled their houses with painted pottery, sculptures, and pretty jewelry.

This type of early temple is called a ziggurat.

Making a piece of pottery

Grinding flour for bread

29

How we know

There are no written records that tell us about the earliest peoples. Archaeologists have to study bones, pots, and anything else left behind by our early ancestors to find out about their everyday lives. First archaeologists dig in the ground to look for clues. Then they study what they have found, sometimes using special scientific equipment.

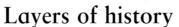

Using science

A scientific method known as radiocarbon dating helps archaeologists find out an object's age. X rays are used to examine mummies without damaging them.

Ice man

In 1991 the 5,300-year-old body of a man was found high in the Alps in Europe. It had been preserved by ice. Scientists who studied the body learned that the man may have been murdered.

Layers of history

The deeper an object is buried, the older it is likely to be. Archaeologists dig carefully to avoid causing any damage. Sometimes they find layers of objects in the order that they were used in history.

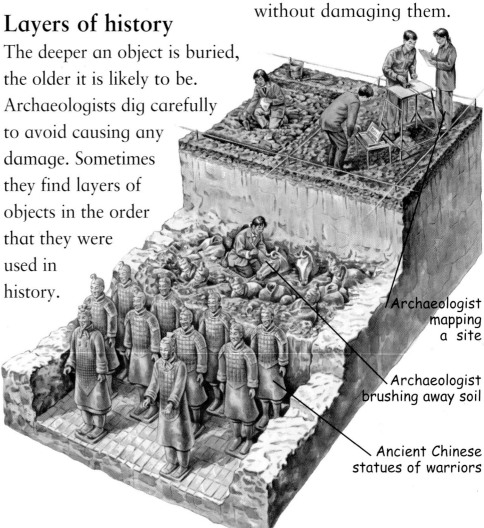

Archaeologist mapping a site

Archaeologist brushing away soil

Ancient Chinese statues of warriors

Glossary

ancestor A dead relative from long ago in history.

ape A hairy mammal that has two arms and two legs and a short tail. Apes can walk upright or on all fours.

archaeologist A person who digs up objects left behind by earlier people and studies them to find out how our ancestors lived.

Australopithecus Apelike animals that lived between five and one million years ago and that showed the first human characteristics.

Bronze Age A period in the history of humans when tools, weapons, and jewelry were made from the metal bronze.

casting A way of making shaped objects, such as weapons, by pouring hot metal into a mold.

crop A plant that is grown by people as food for themselves or their animals.

fertile Land that produces good crops is described as fertile.

fort A settlement or building that is protected by walls and trenches.

Homo erectus The scientific name for our ancestors who lived from 1.8 million years ago and were the first to walk upright.

Homo habilis The scientific name for our ancestors who lived from two million years ago and were the first to make simple tools.

Homo sapiens The scientific name for our most recent ancestors. *Homo sapiens* lived from one million years ago until the present and have developed into modern humans.

Ice age A period of time when much of the earth's surface is covered with ice. There have been a number of ice ages over the past two million years.

The last Ice Age ended 10,000 years ago. The warmer periods of time between ice ages are known as interglacials.

Iron Age A period in the history of humans when tools, weapons, and jewelry were made from the metal iron.

mammoth A type of hairy elephant that lived in the most recent Ice Age but that is now extinct.

Neanderthal Humanlike creatures that lived from 100,000 to 35,000 years ago. They walked upright and made tools.

predators Animals that hunt and prey on other animals are known as predators. Saber-toothed tigers are predators.

species Groups of plants or animals that have similar characteristics.

temple A large building where people gather to pray to a god or gods.

tool An object that is used to carry out tasks. For example, our ancestors used hammering tools to make axes from stones.

Index